CITIES

DALLAS

ABDO
Publishing Company

Nancy Furstinger

visit us at
www.abdopub.com

Published by ABDO Publishing Company, 4940 Viking Drive, Edina, Minnesota 55435. Copyright © 2005 by Abdo Consulting Group, Inc. International copyrights reserved in all countries. No part of this book may be reproduced in any form without written permission from the publisher. The Checkerboard Library™ is a trademark and logo of ABDO Publishing Company.

Printed in the United States.

Cover Photo: Corbis
Interior Photos: AP/Wide World pp. 14, 19, 23, 25, 28; Corbis pp. 1, 5, 6-7, 12-13, 15, 16, 17, 18, 20, 21, 22, 24, 27, 29; Getty Images p. 13; North Wind p. 11

Series Coordinator: Jennifer R. Krueger
Editors: Stephanie Hedlund, Megan Murphy
Art Direction & Maps: Neil Klinepier

Library of Congress Cataloging-in-Publication Data

Furstinger, Nancy.
    Dallas / Nancy Furstinger.
        p. cm. -- (Cities)
    Includes bibliographical references and index.
    ISBN 1-59197-858-0
        1. Dallas (Tex.)--Juvenile literature. I. Title.

F394.D214F87 2005
976.4'2812--dc22

                                                            2004052166

CONTENTS

DALLAS

Dallas is located in north central Texas. After Houston, Dallas is the second-largest city in the state. It is the eighth-largest U.S. city. Dallas is part of a large **urban** area that includes several other Texas cities. This area, along with Fort Worth, is known as the Metroplex.

Dallas began as a two-cabin town on the Trinity River. When the railroad arrived in Dallas, the city grew rapidly. The cotton industry and the Texas oil boom created further growth.

Today, Dallas combines Southwestern charm with big-city style. Once the heart of the cattle range, the city is known for its small-town friendliness. Yet, Dallas also has a **sophisticated** side. It is the **cultural** center of the Southwest.

In all seasons, Dallas offers a choice of activities. The city has the largest state fair in the country. It hosts one of the most popular rodeos in all of Texas. And, Dallas has more shopping centers per person than any other U.S. city.

Dallas's modern skyline rises above the rolling grasslands of north central Texas. Only 30 years after World War II, the population of Dallas had tripled. Today, it is one of the ten largest cities in the country.

DALLAS AT A GLANCE

Date of Founding: **1841**

Population: **1 million**

Metro Area: **384 square miles (995 sq km)**

Average Temperatures:
- **44° Fahrenheit (7°C)** in winter
- **85° Fahrenheit (29°C)** in summer

Annual Rainfall: **30 inches (76 cm)**

Elevation: **450–750 feet (137–229 m)**

Landmarks: **Trinity River, White Rock Lake**

Money: **U.S. Dollar**

Language: **English**

FUN FACTS

John Neely Bryan named his town "for my friend Dallas." However, he never revealed who earned this honor. Many believe the city was named after George Mifflin Dallas. He was the United States vice president from 1845 to 1849.

Dallas's Fair Park was designated as a national historic landmark in 1986.

TIMELINE

1836 - The Republic of Texas is established.

1841 - John Neely Bryan builds a cabin on the Trinity River and starts a town there. He names it Dallas.

1845 - Dallas's citizens vote in favor of the annexation of Texas.

1846 - On March 30, Dallas County is organized; Dallas becomes the temporary county seat in April.

1856 - Dallas is officially recognized as a town by the Texas legislature.

1860 - A fire destroys part of the city.

1870s - The railroad arrives in Dallas.

1930 - Oil fields are discovered in East Texas.

1936 - Dallas hosts the Texas Centennial Celebration, which recognized the state's 100 years of independence from Mexico.

TWO-CABIN TOWN

The area around present-day Dallas has a long history. Native Americans were the first to settle the land. Then in the 1700s, Europeans arrived. Mexico became an independent country in 1821, and Texas was one of its states.

Mexico bordered the expanding United States. Soon, many U.S. citizens began moving to Texas. These citizens did not want to be under Spanish rule. So in 1836, Texas declared itself an independent **republic**.

People continued to move to the Republic of Texas. One of them was John Neely Bryan. In 1841, this Tennessee lawyer built a cabin on the Trinity River in north central Texas. He decided to start a town. He named it Dallas.

Bryan invited others to settle here. By 1843, the town consisted of two log cabins. For a while, Bryan acted as postmaster and store owner. And, his home was the courthouse. Farmers, traders, and **artisans** soon flocked to the area. The town of Dallas grew quickly.

The **Republic** of Texas did not have the money to remain independent. So in 1845, Texas was **annexed** to the United States. Of the 32 Dallas citizens who could vote, 29 said yes to the annexation.

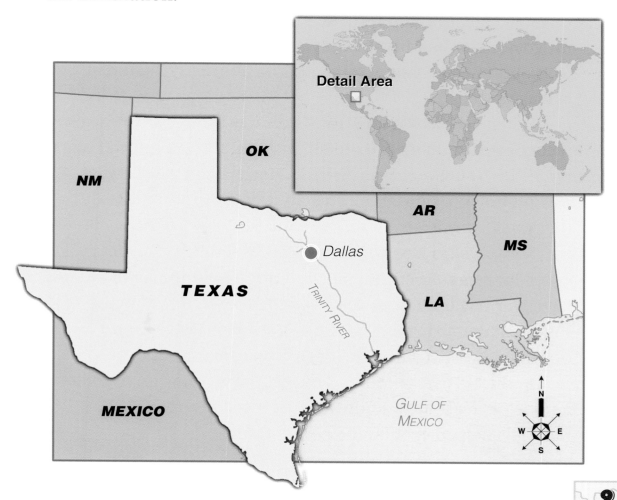

On March 30, 1846, Dallas County was organized. In April, Dallas became the temporary county seat. It officially became the county seat four years later.

During the California gold rush, many people passed through Dallas on their way west. Many Dallasites left to look for gold, including Bryan. He was unsuccessful and returned to Dallas in 1850. Many other people returned to settle in Dallas as well.

Dallas continued to grow. The Texas legislature officially recognized it as a town in 1856. In 1860, a fire destroyed many buildings in the business district. However, most of Dallas was rebuilt in six months. The city was growing so quickly that there were housing shortages.

Soon, Dallas began preparing for war. Dallas County voted for **secession** from the United States in 1861. When the **Civil War** began in June, the city served as a supply center for the Confederate army. After the South lost, Dallas was occupied by Union troops during **Reconstruction**.

In the 1870s, the railroad arrived. The trains made Dallas a trade center for the southwestern United States. The railroads helped expand the cotton trade.

In 1872, the population of Dallas was 7,000. By 1890, that number had increased to 38,000. Dallas was the largest city in Texas at that time. Then, the East Texas oil fields were discovered in 1930. This made the city a center for the oil industry as well.

Following **World War II**, Dallas experienced a period of spectacular growth. The population tripled by 1970. The oil industry declined in the 1980s. But today, Dallas is considered a primary business center in the United States.

A busy railroad depot in Texas in the 1870s

COTTON & OIL

Since the 1800s, cotton and oil have shaped Dallas's **economy**. Today, Dallas remains one of the world's leading cotton markets. However, the oil industry has declined in the past 20 years. Yet, more oil firms have their headquarters in Dallas than in any other U.S. city.

Dallas emerged as a manufacturing city in the 1940s. **World War II** marked the turning point. Planes were needed for the war, so Dallas's aircraft industry grew. Following the war,

One of the world's largest sundials stands at the entrance to the headquarters of Texas Instruments in Dallas. The company started in Dallas in the 1930s and is famous for creating the hand-held calculator.

Neiman Marcus, founded in 1907, is one of the most famous department stores that was started in Dallas.

electronics and computers became a major factor in the Dallas **economy**.

Today, the core of Dallas's economy is retail trade. Dallas is a major fashion center. It is known for the manufacture and wholesale of clothing. The Dallas Market Center is the world's largest wholesale shopping mall.

Dallas is also the leading banking and financial center of the Southwest. The city is the headquarters of more than 100 insurance companies. Dallas is also home to the national center of the American Heart Association.

GOVERNMENT

Dallas is the largest American city operating under the council-manager form of government. This form of government was adopted in 1931.

In this system, Dallas is divided into 14 districts. Each district is represented by a city council member. The term for council members is two years, but they can be re-elected for four terms.

Mayor Laura Miller

The council appoints a city manager as chief administrative and executive officer. However, the 14 council members and the mayor are the policy-making body.

The mayor is elected every four years. In 2002, Laura Miller was elected to this position. She previously served as a member of the Dallas City Council. Mayor Miller is interested in improving services, such as parks, for all Dallasites.

Old City Park is a living history museum in the heart of Dallas. The museum has preserved 38 buildings from the Civil War era and provides educational programs about the history of Dallas.

TRAVEL CENTER

A freeway overpass in Dallas

Dallas is the major transportation center of the Southwest. It is also a stopping point between the four largest population centers on the continent. This makes Dallas-Fort Worth International Airport one of the country's busiest airports.

Getting around Dallas can be a challenge. The city is a confusing tangle of streets. Dallas began as many small, separate towns. When the small towns became one city, officials kept many of the original street names. So, one street can have several different names along its entire length.

Dallas has been slow at developing a public transportation system. Travel by bus and light-rail has improved. However, many areas of the city are still without public transportation. It is almost impossible to get around without a car. This contributes to heavy traffic.

But unlike Dallas's streets, its freeways are easy to navigate. In fact, there is a major freeway on each side of Dallas.

An airport tram transports travelers at Dallas-Fort Worth International Airport. This airport links the four largest cities in North America. They are New York, Los Angeles, Chicago, and Mexico City.

HOT & COLD

The three forks of the Trinity River join near downtown Dallas. For much of the city's early history, flooding caused a lot of damage along the river. So in 1930, the city built a 50-foot (15-m) earthen **levee** to hold back the river.

Despite flooding issues, Dallas didn't always have enough water. The city had problems with water shortages until the late 1950s. Then, Dallas built new **reservoirs** to solve these problems. The lands surrounding the reservoirs now serve as recreation areas.

In addition to the Trinity River, White Rock Lake is another body of water near Dallas.

Dallas's southern location causes its weather to have hot and cold extremes. The city has long winters, but they are mild. However, cold

A rare snowstorm in Dallas

fronts called northeasters strike now and then. Summers are very hot. In 1980, Dallas reported a record high of 113 degrees Fahrenheit (45°C) on June 26 and 27.

Spring and fall are the shortest seasons. They are also considered the most pleasant. However in the spring, severe storms often occur. These storms bring lightning, rain, hail, and sometimes tornadoes.

DALLASITES

Since its early years, Dallas has attracted a variety of citizens. French **artisans** arrived in 1855. When the **Civil War** ended, many African Americans moved to the city. Industry was booming compared to much of the Southwest. So, many Southerners moved to Dallas to rebuild their fortunes.

Today, Dallas is a blend of many nationalities. Some Dallasites are Native Americans. Others are Asian and Latino **immigrants**. After English, Spanish is the most common language.

Because of the variety of people, many religions are found in Dallas. The city has congregations of Catholics, Jews, and **Muslims**. However, Baptists are the most common religious group.

A traditional Texas breakfast of eggs, hash browns, bacon, and biscuits and gravy

The Reunion Tower was built in 1978 as part of the Dallas Hyatt Regency Hotel. It was named for La Réunion, a colony of immigrant French artists founded in the 1850s.

Most Dallasites eat out four times a week, which is the third-highest rate in the country. Southwestern cuisine, or Tex-Mex, is the regional flavor. Items such as chicken-fried steak and enchiladas can be found on most menus. Dallas also has plenty of steak houses and barbecue shacks.

LA RÉUNION

Some of Dallas's first Europeans came from a settlement called La Réunion. In 1855, a group of artists and musicians from France planned a farming community. They wanted to create a utopian, or ideal, society. But, their vision was doomed because these settlers weren't farmers. The land they chose, across the river from Dallas, was not fit for farming. The group split up in 1857. Some moved to Dallas and established the artist community that exists in the Deep Ellum neighborhood today.

A residential home in Dallas

Dallas has many historic housing neighborhoods. Swiss Avenue has more than 200 restored homes. Restored redbrick houses are found in the West End Historical District as well.

However, single-family homes represent the majority of houses in Dallas. Most have wood frames or are made of brick or stone. Ranch-style homes are popular, too. People also live in apartments and condominiums.

The Dallas Independent School District is the twelfth-largest school district in the nation. More than 161,000 students are registered.

Dallas students attend public elementary and secondary schools. There are also about 30 private schools in the city. Many of these private schools offer religion-based education.

After high school, students may go to college. Southern Methodist University is the oldest and most well-known campus in Dallas. It opened in 1911. Other campuses include DeVry Institute of Technology, Bishop College, and the University of Dallas.

AMERICA'S TEAM

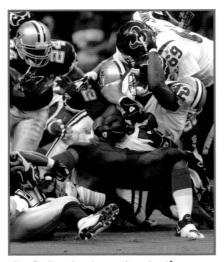

The Dallas Cowboys play the Houston Texans at Reliant Stadium in Houston.

Dallasites are big sports fans. With all-star teams in football, baseball, and basketball, Dallas offers plenty of games throughout the year.

The Dallas Cowboys have been Super Bowl winners five times. Their overwhelming popularity with sports fans across the country earned them the nickname "America's team." The Cowboys play in Texas Stadium.

The Texas Rangers attract huge crowds at Ameriquest Field. In 2004, the Rangers became the second team in Major League Baseball to have its starting infielders hit more than 20 home runs each.

Basketball fans can catch a game at the American Airlines Center. This is where the Dallas Mavericks play. The center also hosts the Dallas Stars hockey team.

Two of the nation's best college football teams play each other in the annual Cotton Bowl. Held on New Year's Day, the game is played at Cotton Bowl Stadium in Fair Park.

Another popular Texas sporting event is the rodeo. To start the annual Texas Stampede, cowboys drive cattle through the streets of Dallas. No true Texan can miss this rodeo. It includes a country music concert and the crowning of Miss Texas Stampede.

More than 100 cattle are herded through downtown Dallas to start the annual Texas Stampede.

THINGS TO SEE

One of the most interesting aspects of Dallas is its **architecture**. Fair Park is home to the country's largest collection of **art deco** buildings. Dallas City Hall was designed by architect I.M. Pei. It is shaped like an upside-down triangle.

Dallas also has several arts and entertainment neighborhoods. Deep Ellum was a popular spot for blues music during the early 1900s. Today, there are many clubs and artist hangouts here.

The West End Historical District has many preserved and restored buildings. Old warehouses have been turned into stores and restaurants. The Dallas Arts District is a 17-block area with theaters, museums, a concert hall, and a sculpture garden.

Dallas is known for its **cultural** activities. They include symphony concerts, operas, and ballets. The city also has many museums devoted to art, science, and history.

DEALEY PLAZA

On November 22, 1963, President John F. Kennedy was riding in a motorcade in Dallas when he was assassinated. The shots had come from the sixth floor of a downtown Dallas building. Lee Harvey Oswald was arrested for the murder. Before he could stand trial, Oswald was killed by Jack Ruby.

Dallas still honors President Kennedy's memory. An X marks the spot in Dealey Plaza where the president was killed. There is also a plaque that designates the plaza as a historical landmark. Above the site, the Sixth Floor Museum opened. There, photos and films remember that historic day.

THINGS TO DO

Many of Dallas's events are held in Fair Park. This was the site of the Texas Centennial Celebration in 1936. Many of the **art deco** buildings in Fair Park were constructed specifically for the centennial. The park is also the site of the Texas State Fairgrounds.

The Texas State Fair runs for 24 days each September. Big Tex, a 52-foot (16-m) papier-maché cowboy, greets fairgoers as they enter the park. The fair offers a midway, laser light show, and parade. It also has the largest Ferris wheel in North America. The Texas Star is 212 feet (65 m) tall.

Big Tex drawls, "Howdy, folks," to visitors as they enter the Texas State Fairgrounds.

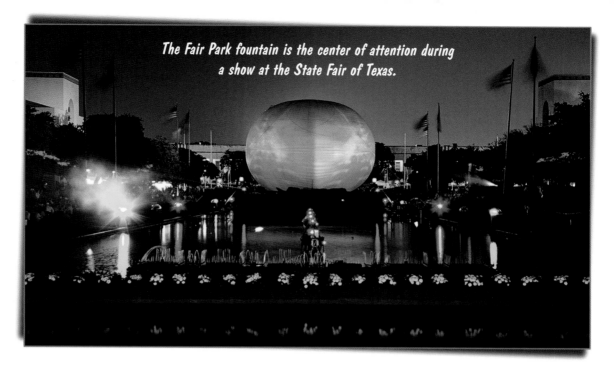

The Fair Park fountain is the center of attention during a show at the State Fair of Texas.

Fair Park attracts visitors even after the fair is over. Many museums dot the site, including the Museum of Fine Arts and the Museum of Natural History. The park overlooks a lagoon that is perfect for a nature walk. Visitors can view wildlife that make their homes near the park.

Visitors can also see other wild animals at Fair Park. The Dallas Aquarium has 6,000 species of marine animals. Visitors can see piranha feedings and jellyfish exhibits. At the Dallas Zoo, baboons, zebras, and okapi roam the Wilds of Africa. People can also see gorillas play or watch endangered tigers.

GLOSSARY

annex - to take land and add it to a nation.

architecture - the art of planning and designing buildings. A person who designs architecture is called an architect.

art deco - a style of the 1920s and 1930s that uses bold shapes and designs.

artisan - a person skilled in a craft or trade.

civil war - a war between groups in the same country. The United States of America and the Confederate States of America fought a civil war from 1861 to 1865.

culture - the customs, arts, and tools of a nation or people at a certain time.

economy - the way a nation uses its money, goods, and natural resources.

immigrate - to enter another country to live. A person who immigrates is called an immigrant.

levee - a ridge of earth built along a river to prevent flooding.

Muslim - a person who follows Islam. Islam is a religion based on the teachings of the prophet Muhammad as they appear in the Koran.

Reconstruction - the period after the Civil War when laws were passed to help the Southern states rebuild and return to the Union.

republic - a form of government in which authority rests with voting citizens and is carried out by elected officials.

reservoir - a natural or human-made place that stores water.
secession - formal withdrawal from an organization.
sophisticated - having worldly knowledge or experience.
urban - of or relating to a city.
World War II - from 1939 to 1945, fought in Europe, Asia, and Africa. Great Britain, France, the United States, the Soviet Union, and their allies were on one side. Germany, Italy, Japan, and their allies were on the other side.

SAYING IT

deco - DEH-koh
Ellum - ELL-uhm
okapi - oh-KAH-pee
reservoir - REH-zuh-vwahr

WEB SITES

To learn more about Dallas, visit ABDO Publishing Company on the World Wide Web at **www.abdopub.com**. Web sites about Dallas are featured on our Book Links page. These links are routinely monitored and updated to provide the most current information available.

INDEX

DATE DUE

SEP 1 1 2006			
JAN 2 3			